Ulysses Press

Published in the United States by:
Ulysses Press
P.O. Box 3440
Berkeley, CA 94703
www.ulyssespress.com

ISBN: 978-1-61243-895-5

Printed in Canada by Marquis Book Printing

2 4 6 8 10 9 7 5 3 1

Illustrations © Metamoki LLC

Distributed by Publishers Group West

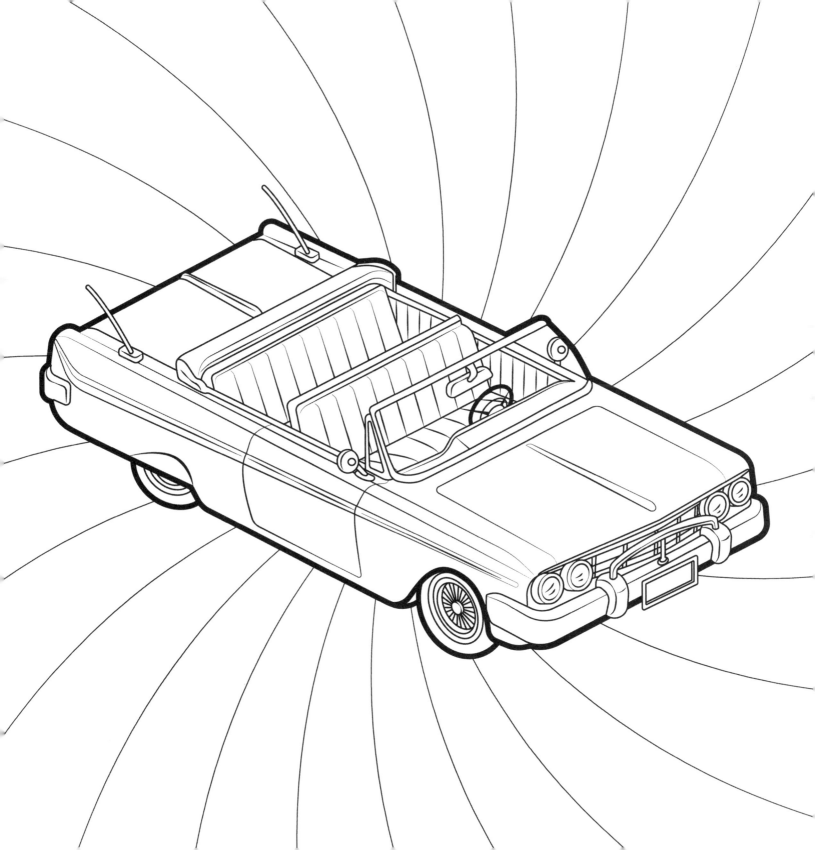

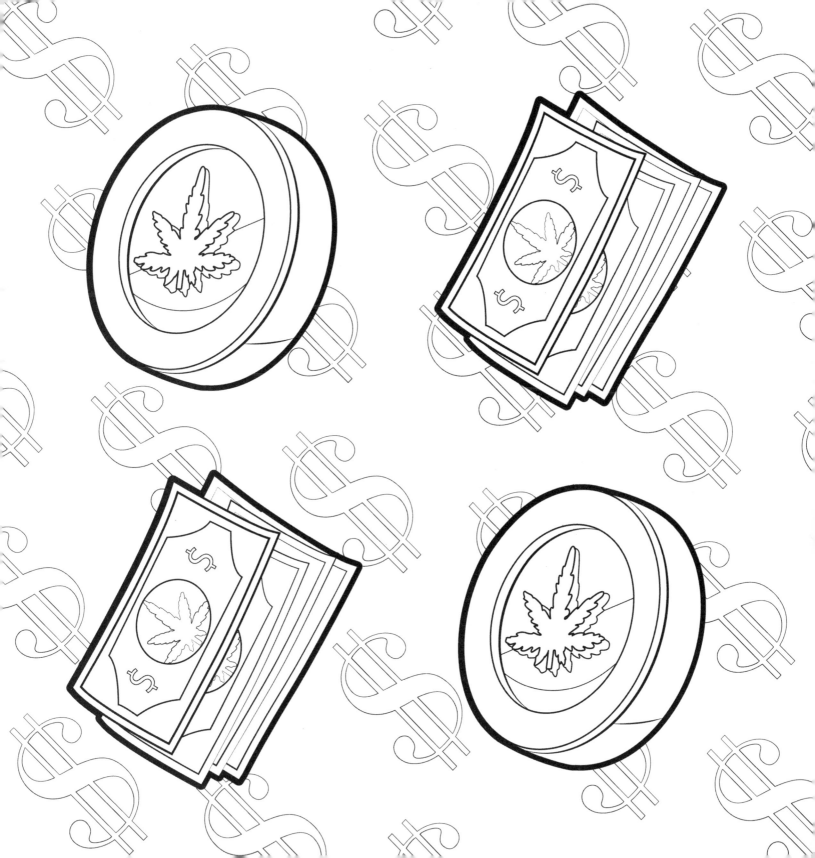

BLACK JACK